GALAPAGOS
WILDLIFE
ADVENTURE TRAVEL GUIDE
BOOK 2025

Brenda J. Smith

Disclaimer

The author and publisher have made every effort to ensure the accuracy and completeness of information in this book. However, they assume no responsibility for errors, omissions, or contrary interpretation of the subject matter herein. This book is intended as a guide and inspiration for travel, and all travel decisions are made at the reader's discretion.

Table of Contents

Introduction

A personal invitation to explore the lovely Galapagos.

As I sit here, reflecting on my own travels through the **Galapagos Islands,** I can't help but be amazed at how these islands, suspended in time, have left an everlasting impact on my heart. To say that the Galapagos Islands are unlike any other place would be an understatement, it's an experience that speaks to you on a deeply intimate level. There is a charm in the air here, something ancient, unspoiled, and pure. It's a location where the natural world shows itself in its purest form, allowing you to watch the dance of evolution firsthand.

When I first arrived, I had no idea what to expect—all I had were legends about enormous tortoises, lively sea lions, and volcanic vistas. But nothing could have prepared me for the stunning beauty and profound calm of the islands. The Galapagos Islands are more than just a tourist attraction; they are a live, breathing example of nature's wonders. Each day here felt like walking into a book, yet the adventure was entirely mine. I followed in **Charles Darwin's** footsteps and discovered not just the islands, but also a fresh perspective on the world.

Now I'd like to offer an invitation to you: come experience the enchantment for yourself. The Galapagos is waiting, eager to unveil its secrets to those who venture beyond the usual tourist routes. From the crystal-clear waters brimming with marine life to the rocky volcanic scenery that depicts the tale of the Earth's evolution, there is something for every visitor. Whether you are a nature lover, an explorer, or simply looking for peace and tranquility, the Galapagos Islands will astound you, as they did me.

How This Guide Will Help in Your Journey

This guide is my way of sharing what I've learned from my personal trips, with insights, ideas, and recommendations to make your trip to the Galapagos as memorable as mine. I've spent numerous hours researching the most recent information, curating experiences that capture the essence of these islands, and offering practical guidance to help you navigate this unique trip.

Turning these pages will reveal more than just statistics and figures; you will discover the Galapagos' soul. I'll take you from the bustling ports of **Santa Cruz** to the peaceful beaches of *Isabela,* snorkeling with sea lions and hiking through volcanic scenery. Along the way, you'll learn about the Galapagos' fascinating people, wildlife, and rich history.

What distinguishes this guide is its focus on sustainability and responsible travel. During my stay here, I've learned the value of maintaining the delicate balance of this environment. It's more than just visiting; it's about leaving the islands as we found them, preserving their beauty for future generations. I've included practical suggestions on how to travel safely and how to help local communities, so that your visit has a good influence.

Whether you're planning a short trip or a longer excursion, this book will be your companion, providing a bespoke experience based on your interests, budget, and travel style. By the end of this book, you will not only have a greater understanding of the Galapagos, but also be well equipped to make the most of your time here.
So pack your luggage, get your camera set, and prepare for an incredible vacation. The Galapagos Islands await, and I promise you that this tour will revolutionize the way you perceive the world.

Chapter 1: Introduction to the Galapagos Islands

1.1 Archipelago Evolution: A Historical Overview

The Galapagos Islands are a living witness to nature's forces, an archipelago where the story of evolution is inscribed across volcanic landscapes, with each rock and ripple of water telling a story of survival and development. These islands, located around 600 miles off the coast of Ecuador, were formed by volcanic eruptions that happened millions of years ago. The result is an archipelago unlike any other in the world, with each island having its own unique ecosystem, wildlife, and history.

The Spanish Bishop Fray Tomás de Berlanga made the first reported discovery of the Galapagos Islands in 1535. The islands did not acquire international recognition until the early nineteenth century, when Charles Darwin paid visits. Darwin's trip to the Galapagos Islands in 1835 was critical to the formulation of his natural selection theory. The diversity of organisms he encountered, each uniquely suited to its island environment, served as the foundation for his evolutionary research. Darwin's findings, particularly with finches and tortoises, altered our view of the natural world.

Today, the Galapagos Islands are both a **UNESCO World Heritage Site** and an Ecuadorian national park. However, its ecological relevance is not limited to the past; it is evolving as the islands deal with the stresses of climate change, invasive species, and human activity. Nonetheless, the islands' remoteness has maintained much of their natural biodiversity, providing a look into the past, frozen in time but constantly evolving. This evolution is what makes the Galapagos so fascinating— everything here has adapted to its particular environment, providing a live demonstration of Darwinian principles at work.

1.2 Why the Galapagos Is Still a Must-See by 2025

By 2025, the Galapagos will surely remain one of the world's most sought-after tourist attractions. The islands' lasting relevance today stems from their unique combination of pure natural beauty, biodiversity, and an unrivaled opportunity to see the ongoing process of evolution. While many sites across the world struggle with over tourism and environmental damage, the Galapagos Islands manage to maintain a tenuous balance. In 2025, the Galapagos will continue to captivate visitors with its stunning species, most of which is found nowhere else on the planet. Imagine snorkeling with sea lions who appear to welcome you into their habitat, or strolling along trails where gigantic tortoises roam freely, unaffected by human presence. The islands are also continually changing, with volcanic eruptions creating new landscapes and unique species reacting to these transitions. Every visit brings something new, whether it's the arrival of fresh sea lion pups, the hatching of endangered bird species, or the discovery of a previously unknown volcanic crater.

What genuinely distinguishes the Galapagos Islands in 2025 is its commitment to sustainability. Conservation efforts are stronger than ever, and the islands remain a world leader in eco-tourism and environmental protection. The implementation of rigorous visiting limitations, protected marine areas, and educational programs guarantees that tourists can enjoy the islands while leaving no detrimental influence. By visiting in 2025, you can help protect this extraordinary site for future generations.

1.3 What Makes the Galapagos So Unique

What actually distinguishes the Galapagos is not only its fauna, but also the character of its environment and ecosystems, which have evolved in beautiful isolation over millions of years. The islands are a living laboratory of nature, allowing you to observe the consequences of evolution in real time. The creatures here aren't shy—sea lions bask on the beaches, **blue-footed boobies** perform their exquisite mating dances, and marine iguanas sunbathe on the rocks, their bodies blending in with the volcanic environment. There is a connection with nature here that is difficult to find anyplace else in the world.

The diversity of ecosystems found in such a tiny region is also astounding. On one island, the scenery is barren and dominated by cacti, while on another, the highlands are lush and covered in mist. The volcanic craters generate distinct microclimates, and the surrounding waters are teeming with marine life, including sharks, rays, and the well-known Galapagos penguin. The contrast between the harsh, spectacular vistas and the fragile ecosystems they support remains with you long after you leave.

But what truly distinguishes the Galapagos is the opportunity to interact with these surroundings in ways that are rarely achievable elsewhere. The islands are meant for exploration, and every visitor has the opportunity to engage with nature on a deep level. Whether you're walking alongside a huge tortoise, seeing a sea lion playfully approach your kayak, or listening to the wind whistle through the volcanic rocks, the Galapagos Islands provide a closeness with nature unlike any other location in the world. It's a place where humans are guests in a much broader, more ancient world—one that humbles and awes in equal parts.

The Galapagos Islands are exceptional not only for their natural wonders, but also for the conservation mentality that infuses all aspects of island life. From eco-lodges that reduce environmental effect to local tour operators committed to sustainability, the islands operate with a great respect for the fragile balance of their ecosystems. This commitment to preservation guarantees that the islands adapt while retaining the core of what makes them so unique.

In short, the Galapagos Islands are more than just a destination; they are a timeless experience that will change your perspective on life, nature, and your surroundings. It's a location where you can not only observe but also participate, connecting with the world in its most real form. And in 2025, it's still as much a must-see as it was when Darwin first stepped onto its shores.

Chapter 2: The Best Time to Visit the Galapagos.

2.1 My Personal Experiences with the Seasons

When I first arrived in the *Galapagos,* I did not give much thought to the timing of my visit. I was simply excited to explore the islands. But as soon as I stepped onto those sun-drenched beaches, I knew that the seasons in the Galapagos greatly influence your experience. What I've learned over the years is that there is no "one-size-fits-all" time to visit; the optimal season is entirely dependent on the type of experience you seek.

- During my first journey, I arrived during the dry season, which spans from *June to November*. The weather was crisp, with bright sunshine and mild winds, especially in the islands' mountains. Standing on the brink of a cliff on Santa Cruz, I recall looking out at the pristine blue ocean extending out in front of me. The dry season also brings cooler waters, which made snorkeling and diving much more enjoyable, especially when encountering frisky sea lions.

- However, during a subsequent visit during the wet season *(December to May),* the islands took on a completely new character. The rain was mild, falling in quick bursts that accentuated the beautiful green scenery. The water warmed up, making it an ideal opportunity to snorkel with marine life. I swam with enormous manta rays, observed schools of tropical fish in the shallows, and marveled at the sight of Galapagos penguins gliding through the water. The contrast between the two seasons was stark, and each had its own appeal.

If you're wondering which season is best, I can tell you: it all depends on your own preferences. Both seasons provide distinct experiences that you do not want to miss. And, if possible, I highly recommend visiting the islands during both seasons, as each provides something unique and spectacular.

2.2 High Season vs. Low Season: Which is better for You

The Galapagos Islands have two unique seasons, each with its own set of advantages: high season and low season. Understanding the variations will help you select when to come based on your priorities, such as avoiding crowds, saving money, or maximizing wildlife interactions.

The Galapagos Islands are busiest during the high season, which lasts from *mid-June to September* and includes the *December holidays.* The islands are famous among travelers from all over the world, especially during school breaks. This translates to more crowded tour boats, buses, and hiking trails. However, the high season also provides numerous advantages. The weather is cold and dry, making it excellent for hiking and other outdoor activities. The fauna is especially busy around this time— marine iguanas congregate in huge numbers, and the islands' famous gigantic tortoises are frequently spotted mating. This is also an excellent season for birdwatching, since many species are nesting and raising their young.

On the other hand, *the low season (late April to early June and November to December)* has less tourists and more quiet scenery. During these months, the weather is warmer and wetter, with brief rains to renew the island's vegetation. The seas are warmer, making it ideal for swimming, snorkeling, and diving. The low season also provides excellent animal viewing opportunities: sea lions and marine turtles are more active, and you may even witness baby turtles or birds hatch. The drawback is that increasing rainfall can cause muddy pathways, particularly in the highlands.

For me, traveling during the off season was a tremendous joy. It felt like I had the whole island to myself. There was something amazing about going along the beaches with no one else around, the sound of the waves breaking in the background, and seeing wildlife up close without being distracted. It was the ideal opportunity to reconnect with nature and immerse myself in the quiet and tranquility of the Galapagos.

So, which season works best for you? If you prefer quieter times, fewer tourists, and the chance to enjoy the islands all to yourself, the low season is excellent. If you don't mind crowds and want to experience the islands' colder, drier environment, the high season may be the perfect time to come. Personally, I believe that balancing both is the best way to really feel the contrast between these two lively seasons.

2.3 Weather and Climate Insights for All Travelers

Understanding the climate of the Galapagos is critical for organizing your vacation. The weather on the islands is principally controlled by two ocean currents: the warm Panama Current, which delivers warmer tropical water from the north, and the cold Humboldt Current, which brings colder water from the south. This confluence of currents produces a distinct climate that varies by season but is reasonably steady year-round.

From December to May, the weather is warm and humid, with temperatures ranging from *77°F to 88°F (25°C to 31°C).* This is the wet season, but the rain is usually irregular, lasting only a few hours or overnight, giving plenty of time for outdoor activities. The warmer seas at this time are great for snorkeling and diving, as you'll see beautiful coral reefs, schools of tropical fish, and possibly even the rare whale shark.

In contrast, from *June to November,* the islands are cooler and drier. Daytime temperatures range from *70°F to 80°F (21°C to 27°C),* but evenings can be pleasantly cold. This is the dry season, marked by mild winds and clear skies. Though the weather is excellent for outdoor activities such as trekking, the sea can be choppy at this time, making aquatic activities such as snorkeling and diving slightly more difficult. However, visibility underwater improves, making it ideal for viewing pelagic fish, hammerhead sharks, and the rare whale.

The climate of the islands varies according to altitude. Even during the summer season, the islands' mountains, such as Santa Cruz's lush woods, can be misty and cold. If you're hoping to tour these places, you'll want to carry a light jacket or sweater, especially early Morning treks. On the other hand, coastal locations are often warmer and sunnier, making them ideal for relaxing on the beach or diving into the crystal-clear waters.

Layers are essential for any season. The weather can change fast, and being prepared can keep you comfortable whether you're hiking through foggy hills or relaxing on a sun-kissed beach. I also recommend taking sunscreen, a hat, and strong walking shoes because there is so much to explore on foot.

Finally, regardless of when you arrive, the Galapagos Islands provide something extraordinary. The seasons on these islands contribute to their dynamic and unique character. Whether you're seeking for wildlife, trekking, or simply taking in the natural splendor, the Galapagos

Islands always have something special to offer. The key is to select the season that best suits your travel objectives, and no matter when you arrive, you'll be rewarded with experiences that will last a lifetime.

Chapter 3: Planning Your Trip: Essentials You Should Know

3.1 Passport, Visa, and Entry Requirements.

Before you set foot in the Galapagos, there are a few preparations you must do to ensure a comfortable sailing experience. As part of Ecuador, the Galapagos Islands have the same entry requirements as the mainland, which include having your passport and comprehending the visa procedures. Fortunately, the process is pretty simple for most travelers.

Tourists traveling from the United States, Canada, the United Kingdom, and many European countries do not require a visa for stays of 90 days or less. All you need is a passport that is valid for at least six months beyond your anticipated travel date. It is also necessary to have proof of return or onward travel, as immigration officers may request it upon arrival in Ecuador.

However, if you intend to stay for more than three months or are traveling from a nation that requires a visa, you must apply in advance. It's always a good idea to check with the nearest Ecuadorian consulate or embassy for the most up-to-date visa requirements before traveling.

When flying to the Galapagos, you'll first arrive in mainland Ecuador, typically in Quito or Guayaquil, where you'll be charged a *Galapagos National Park* entrance fee *(now roughly $100 USD).* This cost is necessary for the preservation of the islands, so include it in your travel budget. After clearing immigration in Ecuador, you will fly to one of two Galapagos airports: *Baltra (for Santa Cruz) or San Cristóbal* (for the eastern islands).

Certain commodities, such as fresh vegetables, seeds, and animal products, cannot be brought to the Galapagos. These laws are tightly enforced to prevent the spread of exotic species. Prepare for baggage checks at the airport and ensure that everything you bring complies with the standards.

3.2 Environmental Regulations: Protecting Islands

The Galapagos Islands are more than just a stunning tourist attraction; they are also an ecological treasure. As a visitor, you must respect the fragile balance of this unique habitat. To safeguard the islands and their residents, Ecuador has imposed stringent environmental laws that all visitors must observe.

One of the first things I observed on my visits was the dedication to maintaining the islands' natural environments. Every visitor must stay within defined areas and obey the "leave no trace" policy. For example, the Galapagos National Park officials implement a policy requiring tourists to explore specific places with a trained naturalist guide. These guides are experts in the islands' flora and fauna, and they guarantee that tourists stay on the designated pathways and do not harm the species.

Wildlife in the Galapagos is unusually fearless of humans, owing to decades of seclusion. However, this also makes it easier to inadvertently cause injury. It is critical to avoid touching, feeding, or provoking the animals. I recall sitting calmly while a sea lion approached me on the beach, but I knew not to interfere— just observing and respecting their space was enough to make the meeting genuinely magical.

Additionally, trash is strictly prohibited. Everything you bring into the islands should be taken with you when you depart. To reduce your environmental effect, bring reusable water bottles instead of single-use plastics. The islands' limited resources make trash management difficult, and eco-friendly travel is critical to preserving the natural beauty and health of the ecosystem.

While it is easy to ignore the minor actions, it is these prudent decisions that will ensure the Galapagos Islands remain a viable destination for future visitors. The more we respect the islands, the longer we may enjoy their splendor.

3.3 Health and Safety Tips: How to Stay Safe While Exploring

Your safety and health are vital when traveling, especially in a remote and unusual destination like the Galapagos. While it is one of the safest tourist locations in the world, you need still take a few precautions to guarantee a smooth vacation.

- Before you travel, make sure you are up to date on standard vaccines such as tetanus, measles, and diphtheria. While no specific immunizations are required for visiting the Galapagos, some people may want to consider hepatitis A or B vaccinations, especially if they will be exposed to local conditions for an extended period of time. Before traveling, always contact with your healthcare professional about any unique health concerns depending on your personal medical history and the activities you intend to engage in.

- In terms of drugs, it's a good idea to pack any necessary prescriptions, especially if you'll be staying for an extended period. While there are pharmacies in the Galapagos, they may not always have the prescriptions you require. Packing a compact first-aid kit containing essentials like as band-aids, antiseptic, and nausea medication is also a smart idea, especially if you intend to spend a lot of time outside or participate in activities such as snorkeling or trekking.

- Even on cloudy days, the sun in the Galapagos may be very bright. I quickly learnt to be diligent in applying sunscreen and wearing protective gear. A wide-brimmed hat and UV-blocking sunglasses are essential. The islands are also notorious for their strong winds, which may quickly dehydrate you, so stay hydrated, especially if you're out on the sea for long periods of time.

- If you plan on trekking, make sure to wear sturdy, comfortable shoes because many of the trails are rough and uneven. The terrain may be rather hot, so carry plenty of water and wear breathable clothing to keep comfortable on extended excursions.

- If you're going snorkeling or diving in the ocean, make sure to use equipment from a respected provider, because safety standards are quite crucial in aquatic activities. I've been on several thrilling dives in Galapagos waters, and while the experience was wonderful, constantly listening to safety briefings and following your tour operator's instructions is vital.

- Mosquitoes, in particular, live in the Galapagos' wet lowlands. While the risk of malaria or dengue fever is low, it's still a good idea to bring bug repellent with DEET, especially if you're going to locations with dense vegetation or near water.

- Finally, while the Galapagos Islands are normally relatively safe, it is always a good idea to keep a check on your valuables. Many regions are isolated, therefore medical facilities may be limited. A solid travel insurance policy is an excellent choice, as it covers both health difficulties and any trip disruptions.

With these safeguards in mind, you can be confident that the Galapagos will provide you with an unforgettable experience that is both safe and healthful. Following the recommendations and respecting local customs will allow you to fully experience the island's beauty without jeopardizing your safety.

Chapter 4: Budgeting for the Galapagos: A Comprehensive Financial Guide

4.1 Determining the Costs: How Much to Budget for Each Day

Planning a vacation to the Galapagos can be intimidating when you total up the expenditures, but with a little planning, you can enjoy this amazing place without breaking the bank. One of the first things I realized while organizing my own vacation was how important it is to understand the breakdown of daily spending. The Galapagos Islands are not a low-cost destination, but you may have an unforgettable experience while staying within your budget.

Here's an approximate daily budget guidance based on my personal experiences, starting with the most basic travel style and progressing to more comfortable options. I recommend setting between *$100 to $250 per day,* depending on your interests and travel style.

- **Low Budget (Backpacker/Basic Traveler):** Between $100 and $120 a day. This includes lodging in hostels or guesthouses, dining at local markets or casual restaurants, and scheduling group trips. The secret to conserving money here is to stick to local restaurants and limit your activities to less expensive excursions.

- **Mid-Range Budget (Comfortable Traveler):** $150–200 per day. This budget covers private hotel accommodations, lunches at midrange restaurants, and a few private tours or boat outings. Expect to stay in eco-lodges or reasonably priced hotels with greater amenities.

- **Luxury budget (high-end traveler):** $250 or more per day. This budget will cover accommodations at upscale resorts, luxury boat cruises, and exquisite food. It's ideal for people looking for personalized guides, luxurious accommodations, and activities such as yacht cruises or diving adventures.

While these figures may appear excessive when compared to other places, they are reasonable for the Galapagos, where everything—from fuel to food—must be delivered from the mainland. Remember that the most of your budget will be spent on lodgings, tours, park entrance fees, and meals.

4.2 Affordable vs. Luxury Experiences

The Galapagos provide a diverse range of experiences, from more inexpensive and environmentally sensitive options to luxury offerings for those seeking the finest of the best. Whether you're on a tight budget or looking to treat yourself, there are numerous ways to adapt your trip to your budget.

During my previous visits, I embraced the inexpensive side of things, staying in local guesthouses and taking budget tours. It was quite fulfilling because it allowed me to interact with people and experience the islands in a very authentic way. For example, I stayed at a modest family-run hotel in Santa Cruz that cost about *$80 per night.* It was modest but pleasant, and the owner, Maria, provided us fantastic recommendations on where to discover the best local food.

In terms of luxury, the Galapagos has some of the world's most premium resorts and private yacht cruises. I had the opportunity to sail aboard a luxury catamaran for a few days during a subsequent visit, and while the experience was absolutely spectacular, it was not for the faint of heart financially. Upscale cruises might cost anything from *$400 to $1,000 per day,* depending on the vessel and tour style. You can also stay at luxury resorts like Finch Bay or Pikaia Lodge, where the service and amenities are first-rate, and every aspect is tailored for comfort and privacy.

Expect to pay between $300 and $500 per night for these kind of lodgings.

Finally, the choice between economical and premium experiences boils down to the type of tourist you are. If you want more immersion and community links, the cheaper option will allow you to explore without sacrificing the authenticity of the Galapagos. If you choose a more lavish and pampered experience, the luxury alternatives will definitely give the indulgence and exclusivity you crave.

4.3 Cost-effective Accommodations, Dining, and Tours

The secret to conserving money on your Galapagos trip is to make wise decisions about where you stay, where you eat, and how you explore. Here's a breakdown of the most cost-effective solutions in each area.

Accommodations:

There are many of low-cost lodging options in the Galapagos. The major islands, such as Santa Cruz, San Cristóbal, and Isabela, include a range of hostels, guesthouses, and basic hotels. My favorite place was a guesthouse in Santa Cruz managed by a charming couple who also served home-cooked meals. Rates began at *$50 per night* for a standard room with private facilities. These low-cost solutions are ideal if you are willing to forego luxury while still seeking comfort and seclusion.

If you're searching for something in the middle, consider eco-lodges or boutique hotels. These typically range from *$100 to $200* per night and provide simple yet modern accommodations with a focus on sustainability. The Scalesia Lodge on Isabela, for example, provides an excellent balance of comfort and environmental responsibility.

Dining:

There is a noticeable distinction between local and tourist-oriented eateries in terms of food. Eating where the locals dine will save you a lot of money. I've had wonderful lunches at local seafood shacks for as little as *$5 to $10* per dish. Street markets also sell fresh fruit, sandwiches, and local pastries for a reasonable price. For a somewhat higher budget, mid-range restaurants serve meals ranging from *$15 to $25,* particularly those selling fresh fish or local delicacies like as ceviche.

Tours:

Group excursions are your greatest option for saving money. I went on many group excursions that cost between *$50 and $80* per person for day outings that included activities such as snorkeling, animal watching, and guided hiking. Some of these tours were on boats that transported us around the islands, allowing us to visit several places in one trip. Private excursions, on the other hand, can range in price from $150 to $300 per day, depending on the activity. It's all about deciding what is most essential to you: a larger experience with other passengers or a more intimate, personalized tour.

4.4 How to Save Without Giving Up on Essential Activities

While the Galapagos Islands can be expensive, there are various methods to stay within your budget while still experiencing the must-see attractions.

Book essential tours ahead of time, such as seeing giant tortoises on Santa Cruz or watching albatross courtship dances in Española. By preparing ahead, you can avoid last-minute price increases and often find a better offer.

Travel in a Group: If you are traveling alone, try joining a group. Many budget tourists collaborate on activities such as boat cruises, snorkeling, and hiking. Splitting costs can help to lower total expenses.

DIY Activities: Some of the best experiences in the Galapagos require no guide or money at all. Simply going through the Santa Cruz highlands to see the tortoises, or hiking to Tortuga Bay on Isabela, are simple activities that provide wonderful animal experiences.

Visit Less-Touristy Islands: While the big islands, such as Santa Cruz and San Cristóbal, are undoubtedly popular, Isabela and Floreana might be cheaper and have fewer tourists. The cost of lodgings and trips is frequently lower, and you may still enjoy the wonder of the Galapagos.

4.5 Recommended Travel Insurance and Currency Tips

Travel insurance is strongly advised when visiting the Galapagos, especially given the islands' isolated position. I always choose complete coverage, which includes medical emergencies, cancellations, and lost luggage. Some policies even include sports like diving and kayaking, which are popular in the Galapagos. Prices vary depending on your age, the length of your vacation, and the type of coverage, but I've found that most policies range between *$50 and $150* for a weeklong trip.

In terms of currency, the Galapagos Islands use the US dollar, which makes things easier for many tourists. ATMs are available in major cities such as **Puerto Ayora on Santa Cruz** and **Puerto Baquerizo Moreno** on San Cristóbal, but I recommend withdrawing cash before visiting smaller islands where ATMs may be limited. Always bring enough cash for little transactions, as some local businesses and restaurants may not accept credit cards.

4.6 A Day-to-Day Example Budget for 2025

Here is an example of a typical 5-day budget for 2025, based on a mid-range budget:

Day One: Arrival in Santa Cruz.

Accommodation costs $120.
Meals cost $30.
Park entrance fee: $100.
Tours/activities: $60 (a half-day guided tour of the highlands).
Total for Day One: $310.

Day 2: Santa Cruz, North Seymour Island

Accommodation costs $120.
Meals cost $30.
Tours/Activities: $100 (day trip to North Seymour with snorkeling).
Total for Day 2: $250.

Day Three: Isabela Island.

Accommodation costs $100.
Meals cost $25.
Tours/Activities: $80 (a snorkeling trip to Los Tuneles).
Total for Day 3: $205.

Day 4: Explore Santa Cruz

Accommodation costs $120.
Meals cost $30.
Tours and Activities: $50 (self-guided tour of Tortuga Bay and Charles Darwin Station).
Total for Day 4: $200.

Day 5: San Cristóbal & Departure

Accommodation costs $120.
Meals cost $30.
Tours
/Activities: $50 (a half-day hike to Lobos Island).
Total for day 5: $200.
Total for five days: $1,165.

This example demonstrates how to balance costs for activities, accommodations, and meals. Keep in mind that this is just one example; you can tailor it to your preferences and whether you want luxury or budget-friendly solutions.

Finally, while the Galapagos can be expensive, with some forethought, you can enjoy all of its beauties on a fair budget. By focusing on the basics and making informed decisions, you will have an unforgettable experience that is well worth the money.

Chapter 5: Traveling to the Galapagos

5.1 How to Find the Best Deals on Flights to the Islands

One of the first things you'll notice about organizing a vacation to the Galapagos is that getting there isn't as simple as booking a direct ticket from your own country. But don't let this discourage you; with a little patience and clever research, you can discover inexpensive flights that won't break the bank.

Your adventure to the Galapagos starts with a flight to mainland *Ecuador*, either *Quito or Guayaquil.* Both towns have excellent international connections, making it easy to obtain flights from major hubs such as New York, *Los Angeles, and Madrid.* When I was planning my vacation, I usually found that traveling to Guayaquil was less expensive than flying to *Quito,* though this can change depending on where you're coming from.

Once in Ecuador, arrange a domestic flight to one of the Galapagos' two airports: *Baltra Island (for Santa Cruz) or San Cristóbal Island (for eastern locations). Avianca, LATAM, and TAME*, an Ecuadorian airline, all conduct regular flights from the mainland to the Galapagos. The flying time is approximately 1.5 to 2 hours. Flights can cost between *$100 and $500* for a round-trip ticket, depending on when you book and how far in advance you purchase your tickets.

Tips for Finding the Best Deals:

- **Book early:** Flights to the Galapagos, particularly during peak seasons, often sell out quickly. I discovered that booking at least 2-3 months in advance allowed me to get a fair deal. Prices tend to increase as the departure date approaches.

- **Use Fare Comparison Websites:** Websites such as Skyscanner and Google Flights are excellent for comparing prices from different airlines and tracking offers. I've used these to locate the best deals on flights from Quito or Guayaquil to the islands.

- **Avoid Peak Travel Times:** If you can, try to avoid traveling during the Galapagos' peak season (December to January and June to August). Flights are frequently more expensive then, so visiting in the shoulder months (April or September) can save you a lot of money.

- **Check with Local Airlines Directly:** Airlines may have unique promotions on their websites that are not available through third-party booking services. I discovered limited-time discounts directly from *LATAM* or *Avianca,* which drastically lowered the cost of my domestic flights.

- When you arrive in Ecuador, note that the Galapagos National Park admission charge ($100 USD) must be paid in cash at any airport. While not included in the cost of your airfare, it is an important factor to consider while budgeting for your trip.

5.2 Transport on the Islands: Ferries, Taxis, and Island Hopping

Getting around the Galapagos Islands differs from most other destinations. With no major highways or public transit, the islands rely on taxis, ferries, and boats to carry visitors between sites. But, despite its isolated location, traveling the Galapagos is rather simple once you understand the ins and outs.

Taxis are widely available on the larger islands, such as *Santa Cruz* and *San Cristóbal,* and the prices are often low. A journey within town or between essential destinations, such as the airport and your accommodation, typically costs between *$5 and $10,* depending on the distance. Be prepared to bargain slightly, especially if you're getting a taxi from a less touristic neighborhood. I discovered that most drivers were really polite and eager to negotiate reasonable pricing, especially if you went during the off-season.

Ferries are the most popular mode of transportation for long distance travels between islands. These boats mainly travel between the principal islands of *Santa Cruz, Isabela*, and *San Cristóbal*. The ferries are reasonably priced, ranging from $25 to $35 per passenger each way. The travel can take anything from 1 to 2.5 hours, depending on your starting place and destination. Booking your ferry tickets in advance isn't always necessary, but I'd recommend it if you're traveling during high seasons, when vessels might fill up quickly. I discovered that booking through your hotel or tour operator is the most effective approach to obtain a seat.

While traveling between islands is relatively simple, it is not always comfortable. The waters around the Galapagos may be rough, and I've had my share of rocky ferry rides. But it's all part of the journey, and the sights from the boat made any pain worthwhile! If you are prone to motion sickness, I recommend taking seasickness medications, which can come in handy during stormy voyages.

If you want to explore the more distant portions of the islands, you can rent kayaks or paddleboards, particularly on *Isabela* and *Santa Cruz*. Kayaking in crystal-clear waters teeming with marine life was one of the most unforgettable experiences I had in Galapagos.

5.3 Tips for Airport Transfers to Your Hotel

Arriving in the Galapagos and finding your way to your hotel might be simple if you plan beforehand. Both Baltra and San Cristóbal airports are modest and well-organized, with obvious signage guiding passengers to cabs and shuttle services. Here's a rundown of what to expect, as well as some advice for a seamless and easy transfer.

From Baltra Airport, Santa Cruz:

Baltra is located on a small island off the coast of *Santa Cruz*, and hotels are not directly accessible from the airport. Upon arrival, take a 10-minute bus journey to the *Itabaca Channel*, where ferries pass to the main island of Santa Cruz. Once on the opposite side, cabs are readily accessible to transport you to communities such as Puerto Ayora, where the majority of accommodations are located. Taxi rides from the *Itabaca Channel* to *Puerto Ayora* often cost between *$20 and $25*. Pre-arranging transports through my hotel proved to be far more convenient. Many hotels will offer this service for an extra price, making the process much more convenient.

From the San Cristóbal Airport:

San Cristóbal's airport is situated on the outskirts of the main town, *Puerto Baquerizo Moreno*. It's only a 10- to 15-minute drive into town, and cabs are accessible directly outside the terminal. A regular journey to your hotel will cost between *$5 and $10*. Unlike *Baltra,* there is no ferry to take, thus getting to your destination is much easier. However, if you're staying in a more remote location or traveling during peak hours, you should double-check transportation availability ahead of time.

Pre-arranged Transfers:

I discovered that arranging transfers through my hotel or tour organizer was the most efficient method to assure a seamless arrival. Many Galapagos resorts provide airport shuttles as part of their services. Booking these in advance always saved me time, and I knew there would be a driver waiting for me when I arrived. This is especially beneficial if you are traveling with a large amount of luggage or want to avoid the stress of haggling with taxi drivers after a lengthy flight.

Finally, because you'll be arriving in an archipelago, your bags may be subjected to further screening for items such as fresh fruits, seeds, and animal products in order to safeguard the islands' ecosystem. Keep these regulations in mind and follow the instructions to guarantee a smooth arrival.

Getting to the Galapagos and exploring the islands are all part of the adventure. While it may be more complicated than simply arranging a flight to a standard destination, the effort is well worth it. Once you've landed, the beauty of the islands and the opportunity for adventure will make the entire trip worthwhile.

Chapter 6: Accommodation Options to Stay in Galapagos

6.1 Favorite Hotels and Lodges, From Budget to Luxury

There are accommodations in the Galapagos for every type of traveler. Whether you are a budget-conscious backpacker or a luxury-seeking traveler, the islands have a variety of options to meet your needs. Having spent time on several of the big islands, I can attest that where you stay may greatly influence your experience. Allow me to walk you through some of my favorite spots, ranging from budget-friendly to luxurious.

Budget-Friendly Stays:

I adore the appeal of small, locally owned guesthouses and eco-friendly hotels in **Santa Cruz** and **San Cristóbal.** One of my favorite low-cost accommodations is **Hostal Darwin** in **Puerto Ayora**, Santa Cruz. It's a low-cost, no-frills option that provides a clean room and a comfortable bed for roughly **$40-$60** each night. The true charm of this establishment, however, is the friendliness of the family who manages it—they will make you feel like a member of the local community. It's also within walking distance of the harbor, making it convenient to explore Puerto Ayora.

Hotel San Vicente in San Cristóbal is another excellent affordable choice. I stayed here for a few days on my first trip to the islands, and it provided everything I needed: modest, comfortable rooms with air conditioning, a nice courtyard, and polite service. Prices start around *$60 per night.* It's a short walk from the airport and an excellent base for exploring the island's highlights, including the well-known Kicker Rock snorkeling location.

Mid-Range Comfort:

If you're ready to pay a little more for more comfort, there are some excellent mid-range alternatives. The Galapagos Safari Camp on Santa Cruz Island, for example, was a particular highlight for me. This glamping experience, located on a hillside overlooking the archipelago, features huge, luxurious tents with private bathrooms, breathtaking views, and a distinct ambiance that combines nature with comfort. Prices start at *$250 per night,* but the feeling of being immersed in nature while still having access to modern luxuries is well worth the money.

Another excellent mid-range alternative is *Hotel Silberstein* on Santa Cruz, which provides excellent service and a lovely outdoor pool for a modest *$150-$180/night.* This family-run house is a short walk from Puerto Ayora, and its central location allows you to easily explore the town and organize activities such as boat trips or turtle viewing.

Luxury Retreats:

For those looking to splurge, the Galapagos Islands do not disappoint. *Pikaia Lodge*, located on a volcanic mountain on Santa Cruz Island, is one of the most luxurious resorts I've ever visited. Prices here begin about *$600 per night,* and for good reason: the rooms are gorgeous, the service is flawless, and you have access to private guides for personalized island tours. The lodge provides all-inclusive packages that include meals, excursions, and transfers. Staying here feels like being on a private retreat, with every detail planned to create a relaxing, delicious experience.

If you're seeking for an extraordinary sea adventure, The *Eclipse Yacht* provides luxury cruises that allow you to visit various islands in maximum comfort. Cabins start at *$1,000* a night and include guided tours, exquisite cuisine, and everything you need to fully enjoy the Galapagos' natural wonders.

6.2 Distinctive Stays: Eco-Lodges and Sustainable Accommodations

The Galapagos Islands are well-known for its remarkable fauna and pristine environment, and many of the island's accommodations are dedicated to protecting it. Many of the lodges emphasize sustainability, and staying in an eco-lodge can be an unforgettable experience in and of itself.

Scalesia Lodge on Isabela Island was one of my favorite eco-friendly accommodations. This all-inclusive eco-lodge is meant to reduce environmental effect, and its remote location ensures you're surrounded by nature at all times. The resort provides magnificent tented accommodations with stunning views of the surrounding forest and wildlife. Prices are slightly more, around *$300-$450* per night, but it's a calm, green retreat where you can eat organic meals created with locally sourced ingredients.

Angermeyer Waterfront Inn, located on Santa Cruz, has a similar eco-conscious feel but with amazing ocean views. It's a little more rustic, but it still has warm accommodations, sustainable methods, and a focus on giving guests a genuine and environmentally responsible experience. This inn is ideal for people seeking a calmer, laid-back experience while still feeling the luxury touch.

What makes eco-lodges unique?

The benefit of staying in an eco-lodge is that you may interact with the Galapagos environment in a meaningful way. You'll be invited to take part in activities such as guided nature walks, wildlife conservation projects, and farm visits. The emphasis is not just on luxury, but also on helping to preserve the islands. You'll feel like you're making a difference while also enjoying the beauty and serenity of this one-of-a-kind location.

6.3 Advantages and Disadvantages of Staying in Santa Cruz, Isabela, or San Cristóbal

When determining where to stay in the Galapagos, one of the most crucial considerations is which island—or islands—will serve as your base. Each of the main islands has an own character, and where you stay can influence the types of activities you can do as well as your overall experience. I spent time on each of the big islands, and here are the advantages and disadvantages of each.

Santa Cruz Island (Puerto Ayora)

Pros:
- The most developed island, offering a diverse choice of lodgings, restaurants, and activities.

- Access to the renowned **Charles Darwin Research Station,** where you can learn about conservation efforts and witness newborn tortoises.

- Convenient access to adjacent islands such as **North Seymour** and **Bartolomé,** perfect for day getaways.

- A lively town vibe with a variety of shopping, dining, and nightlife opportunities.

Cons:

- The most crowded island, especially during high season, thus it might feel touristic at times.

- Can be more expensive than *Isabela* or *San Cristóbal,* particularly for lodging.

Isabela Island (Puerto Villamil)

Pros:

- Known for its natural beauty and slower pace, it is ideal for people seeking peace.

- Amazing activities include snorkeling with sea lions at *Los Tuneles* and hiking up *Sierra Negra Volcano.*

- Beautiful, untamed beaches with a peaceful, low-key vibe.

Cons:

- While there are fewer food and lodging options than in Santa Cruz, there is still plenty to enjoy.

- Ferries from *Santa Cruz* to *Isabela* can be bumpy and occasionally delayed.

San Cristobal Island (Puerto Baquerizo Moreno)

Pros:

- One of the archipelago's most historic islands, having a relaxed atmosphere and smaller villages.

- Close to the breathtaking Kicker Rock, a must-see for divers and snorkelers.

- A fantastic place for nature enthusiasts, with sea lions usually seen lounging about the harbor area.

Cons:
- Smaller and calmer than Santa Cruz and Isabela, with fewer amenities and entertainment alternatives.

- A little distance from some of the more renowned attractions, but still an excellent base for touring.

6.4 Booking Tips and Hidden Gems for 2025

Booking your stay in the Galapagos does not have to be stressful if you follow a few easy guidelines and keep an eye out for hidden gems.

- **Book in Advance:** As I previously stated, the Galapagos Islands may get crowded, especially during peak season. Booking your lodgings several months in advance, especially for more popular lodges and hotels, guarantees you the greatest prices and availability.

- **Look Beyond the primary Islands:** While Santa Cruz, Isabela, and San Cristóbal are the primary tourist destinations, I strongly recommend staying on smaller, less-visited islands such as *Floreana or Genovesa.* These islands are less populated and provide distinct experiences. For example, Floreana Lodge is a small eco-friendly facility with only a few rooms that provides wonderful isolation and access to pure environment.

- **Consider Package Deals:** Many tour operators and hotels in the Galapagos Islands have all-inclusive packages that include lodging, meals, and island excursions. This can be an excellent alternative for streamlining your trip arrangements and saving money on tours. Packages frequently include discounts for lengthier stays.

The Galapagos boasts a diverse selection of housing alternatives, from simple guesthouses to luxury resorts, so there are plenty of possibilities to suit your budget and preferences. Whether you want to immerse yourself in nature at an eco-lodge, experience the luxury of a high-end resort, or prefer the simplicity of a local guesthouse, you'll find something to fit your needs. Your choice of accommodation will have a direct impact on your vacation, so take your time finding the ideal location that meets your travel objectives.

Chapter 7: Best Restaurants in Galapagos

7.1 Tasting the Islands, My Culinary Journey

One of the unexpected pleasures of visiting the Galapagos Islands was discovering the local food. Because of the islands' remote location, many items are locally obtained, and the fishing industry is thriving, allowing you to enjoy some of the freshest seafood you've ever had. My gastronomic adventure around the Galapagos was more than just eating; it was about connecting with the islands' distinct personality through their cuisine. Each meal, whether in a noisy restaurant or a peaceful seaside café, felt like a tiny celebration of the islands' abundant marine and agricultural riches.

From the bustling streets of **Puerto Ayora** to the quieter parts of **Isabela Island,** I discovered that dining in the Galapagos is a cultural experience unto itself. Local chefs combine fresh fish with tropical fruits and vegetables to create flavors that reflect the island's natural abundance. Allow me to walk you through some of my favorite culinary experiences, from fancy dining to simple street cuisine, so you may make the most of your meals while seeing this incredible island.

7.2 Best Seafood in the World: Where to Eat It

As one might think, seafood takes center stage in Galapagos cuisine, and with good cause. The waters around the islands are filled with an astonishing variety of fish and shellfish, and it's not just the flavor that distinguishes this seafood—it's the freshness. I vividly recall the first time I tried ceviche in the Galapagos. The fish was caught that morning, and it had a richness and depth of flavor I'd never tasted before. Whether for lunch or dinner, seafood is an important element of the Galapagos experience.

The "Best" Ceviche: One of my favorite locations to eat ceviche was *IL Giardino* in *Puerto Ayora*, Santa Cruz Island. This charming, family-owned restaurant combines traditional Ecuadorian cuisine with a touch of Italian flair. Their ceviche de pescado (fish ceviche) is exceptional, crafted with freshly caught fish, zesty lemon, and a peppery kick that made my taste buds sing. Prices range from *$12 to $18* for a big serving.

The Rock in Puerto Baquerizo Moreno on *San Cristóbal Island* serves delicious seafood. I got the opportunity to try their lobster and shrimp, which were both wonderfully grilled and delivered with a side of vivid, locally sourced vegetables. The atmosphere is relaxed, with a view of the port, and the pricing are affordable given the quality, with most dishes ranging between *$15 and $25.*

Seafood Feasts at **Red Mangrove** in **Puerto Ayora** provide another wonderful dining experience. It's an ideal site to watch the sunset while eating tuna sashimi or a hefty seafood plate. The restaurant focuses on fresh, sustainable seafood, and the staff is eager to explain where each product originates from. Expect to pay between **$25 and $40** for a seafood entrée, but believe me, it's worth every penny.

For the freshest catch and the most authentic Galapagos seafood experience, seek out places that advertise locally sourced fish. Many of the best restaurants will proudly display the names of the fisherman who provide their ingredients, adding another degree of appreciation for the dish.

7.3 Local Delights: Must-Try Food and Drinks

The Galapagos Islands are most known for their animals, but they also have a diverse and wonderful food. While seafood is the main attraction, there are a few regional specialties worth trying when you come. These traditional meals are a unique combination of indigenous Ecuadorian ingredients, coastal influences, and the island's agricultural riches.

Encebollado: This is the greatest comfort food for natives, and after trying it, I understood why.

Encebollado is a hearty fish stew that includes albacore tuna, tomatoes, onions, and a delicious broth. The meal is commonly served with chifles (fried plantain chips) and lime. It's the ideal lunch to start the day or to enjoy after an afternoon of touring. *Café de la Playa* at *Puerto Baquerizo Moreno* on *San Cristóbal* is a great site to try it, as the stew is presented with a local flavor. Expect to pay between *$7 and $10.*

Langosta (Lobster): Lobster is another Galapagos specialty that appears on many menus. One evening, I went to *The Galapagos Deli* in *Puerto Ayora* and had the most soft and succulent lobster I've ever had. It was expertly grilled and presented with a zesty lemon butter sauce. While lobster can be expensive *($25-$35 per plate),* it's a worthwhile treat if you enjoy seafood.

Patacones: Fried green plantains are a popular snack or side dish in Ecuador and the Galapagos. *Patacones,* which are crispy on the outside but soft on the inside, are commonly served with a tangy dipping sauce. I found myself munching on them regularly, whether they were served alongside a bowl of ceviche or as a side dish to my main course.

Drinks to Try: Don't forget to try some of the Galapagos' beverages. Ecuador is well-known for its fresh fruit juices derived from tropical fruits such as passionfruit, guava, and tamarillo. I definitely recommend having a glass of jugos naturales at any local café. For something more potent, try Canelazo, a warm, spiced cocktail blended with cinnamon, sugar, and aguardiente (a sugarcane-based alcohol).

Coffee: Another Galapagos feature that surprised me was the island's coffee. The Galapagos has a tiny but expanding coffee industry, with locally grown beans available in cafes throughout the islands. I found the coffee to be rich, smooth, and full-bodied, especially when combined with a slice of pan de yuca.

7.4 Dining on a Budget: Affordably priced options with authentic flavors

While dining in the Galapagos can be costly, particularly in tourist-heavy regions such as Puerto Ayora, there are lots of inexpensive and delicious options if you know where to look. Most neighborhood eateries and street food vendors serve high-quality meals at reasonable prices. Here are some of my favorite low-cost restaurants that deliver true Galapagos cuisine without emptying your wallet:

Café de la Mar in *Puerto Ayora* is a terrific budget restaurant where you can get a superb fish soup or grilled fish for $8-12. The café provides a relaxed ambiance with views of the port, making it ideal for a leisurely lunch.

La Garrapata is an excellent choice for seafood lovers on a budget. Located in Puerto Ayora, this modest family-run restaurant delivers enormous amounts of fried fish, ceviche, and other seafood specialties for *$10-$15 per.*

The relaxed atmosphere and good service make it a local favorite.

Street Food: As you roam around the islands, you'll come across a variety of food trucks and street sellers selling delicious snacks such as empanadas (savory turnovers stuffed with meat or cheese) and *bocadillos* (local sandwiches). These are ideal for a fast bite while on the run and often cost *$3-$5.* I frequently grabbed a hot empanada de camarón (shrimp empanada) to eat on my afternoon stroll.

Take advantage of daily specials: Many restaurants offer *menu del día* (set lunch menus), which often include a soup, main entrée, and drink for a fraction of the price of à la carte items. I discovered that these daily specials were an excellent way to try traditional foods at a lesser cost, frequently for about *$6-$10 per meal.*

The Galapagos Islands are more than simply spectacular fauna and breathtaking scenery; they also provide a rich and diverse culinary experience that should not be missed. From the finest seafood to traditional Ecuadorian meals and delightful tropical drinks, the islands' food scene reflects the natural splendor that surrounds them. Whether you're enjoying in a sophisticated dining experience or grabbing a quick lunch from a street vendor, you'll undoubtedly discover flavors that delight and memories that last long after your visit.

Chapter 8: The Galapagos Wildlife Experience

8.1 My Close Encounters: Getting Up Close to the Famous Residents

In terms of wildlife, the Galapagos Islands are unlike anything else on Earth. As I toured the archipelago, I discovered that the actual enchantment of these islands is not only in the breathtaking scenery, but also in the possibility to come up close to animals that are both distinctive and courageous. Unlike many other sites where wildlife is elusive or shy, the critters here appear unconcerned about human presence. It's as if the animals know they're in a safe refuge, and they often approach you with curiosity and wonder.

Marine Iguana

My first intimate contact with a marine iguana occurred on Isabela Island's rugged shores. These amazing critters, which can plunge into the ocean to hunt for algae, have no fear of humans. As I stood motionless on the sand, one of these prehistoric-looking reptiles lumbered up to me, glaring at me as if to say, *"Welcome to my world."* I was captivated, and this close encounter was only the beginning.

Galapagos Giant Tortoise

On **Santa Cruz Island**, I had an equally remarkable encounter with one of the island's most recognizable inhabitants: the Galapagos giant tortoise. The tortoises are extremely sluggish moving, but they emanate an ancient serenity that is difficult to ignore.

Charles Darwin Research Station

I visited *the Charles Darwin Research Station* and got the opportunity to witness both adult tortoises and baby hatchlings. Watching them travel in their own leisurely pace, I couldn't help but feel admiration and duty to safeguard these ancient creatures.

Gardner Bay

One of my favorite experiences was snorkeling off Gardner Bay on Española Island with playful sea lions. These fascinating marine mammals are known for their intelligence and curiosity, and it didn't take long for one to touch my camera lens, almost as if it wanted to join in the fun. The delight of seeing a sea lion swim circles around me is something I'll never forget, and it's experiences like these that make the Galapagos feel like a living dream.

8.2 Wildlife Watching Tips: The Best Times and Locations

The best thing about wildlife watching in the Galapagos is that you don't have to spend days in a safari car or on an expedition to see beautiful animals. If you're walking along a Wildlife encounters are a natural part of everyday life here, whether on the beach, trekking to a volcano crater, or snorkeling in crystal-clear seas. However, if you want to observe specific animals or participate in certain activities, you should know the ideal times and locations for each species.

- **Marine Iguanas:** These ancient-looking reptiles can be seen on practically each island, although Isabela and Fernandina provide some of the greatest viewing possibilities. The greatest time to see them is in the morning, when they are sunbathing on the rocks to warm themselves in the sun. If you wish to capture them diving for food, the dry season (June to November) is usually the best time to do it.

- Tortoises in the Galapagos are most commonly seen on the *Santa Cruz* and *San Cristóbal islands.* My most memorable encounters were at *the El Chato Tortoise Reserve* in *Santa Cruz,* where I could stroll right up to these slow-moving giants. Tortoises are more active during the wet season *(December to May),* which is also when they mate. However, they can be seen all year in the highlands, where the milder climate is ideal for them.

- **Sea Lions:** Sea lions can be found all around the Galapagos, from San Cristóbal's beaches to Floreana's rugged coastline. I discovered them in abundance at **Gardner Bay** on **Española Island,** where their lively behavior makes for some of the most entertaining wildlife watching. Sea lions are active all year, so the ideal time to see them is anytime. However, January to March is prime breeding season, making it an ideal time to see pups.

- **Birdwatching:** The Galapagos are a birdwatcher's dream, with hundreds of indigenous species. If you want to observe the famed Darwin's finches, I recommend visiting the Santa Cruz highlands or the forests of **San Cristóbal.** These finches are more visible during the dry season (June to November), however birds such as the Galapagos hawk and blue-footed boobies can be spotted throughout the year. *Genovesa Island,* often known as *"Bird Island,"* is the ideal place to watch *frigate birds* and *Nazca boobies.* Thousands of seabirds nest and fly about the cliffs.

- **Whale Watching:** While the Galapagos are most recognized for its terrestrial and marine wildlife, whale watching is also a fantastic experience. I got the opportunity to observe humpback whales off the *coast of Española* during their migration phase from *June to September.* During this period, the waters are dense with migrating whales, and sightings are common.

8.3 How to Respect and Protect the Unique Ecosystem.

The Galapagos Islands are a fragile ecosystem that, while a wildlife paradise, also requires human respect and care. During my visit, I was struck by the importance of sustainability, as every tour guide and local I encountered highlighted the need to protect this natural marvel for future generations. There are rigorous laws in place, and for good reason: these islands have a unique balance of life that cannot be found anywhere else on the earth.

Here are a few important rules to follow during your vacation to the Galapagos to help safeguard the environment and its inhabitants.

- **Stay on Designated Trails:** Whether hiking or walking through a reserve, always use defined trails. This reduces the likelihood of trampling sensitive ecosystems or disrupting wildlife habitat.

- **Maintain a Respectful Distance from Animals**: While Galapagos animals are extremely tolerant of human presence, it is still vital to keep a respectful distance. Avoid touching or feeding any animals because it can change their natural behavior and upset their way of life.

- **Don't Collect Souvenirs:** While it may be tempting to take home a piece of the Galapagos, it is forbidden to remove anything from the islands, including shells, rocks, and feathers. The islands are protected, and removing natural items may disturb the environment.

- **Avoid Introduced Species:** When visiting the islands, take sure not to introduce non-native species such as seeds, plants, or insects. These could jeopardize the islands' delicate natural equilibrium. Before entering the national parks, have your bags examined for any foreign materials.

- Use Eco-Friendly Products: In a country where nature reigns supreme, it's critical to use biodegradable sunscreen, avoid plastic bags, and practice responsible trash disposal. The

Galapagos Islands are devoted to sustainability, and as visitors, we can help by being environmentally responsible at all times.

8.4 Top Guided Tours for Wildlife Photography and Bird Watching

Guided tours are one of the greatest ways to get the most out of your wildlife encounter in the Galapagos. The islands are so rich in natural wonders that hiring an expert guide will not only broaden your awareness but also help you locate animals you might otherwise miss. Whether you're a novice wildlife photographer or a seasoned birdwatcher, a good guide can help you catch the perfect shot or identify a rare species.

Galapagos Wildlife Photography Tours: Several local businesses, including *Galapagos Safari Camp* and Galapagos Travel, provide specialised wildlife photography tours. These tours are led by skilled photographers who understand the finest locations for unusual images and how to approach animals without upsetting them. I took a photography tour on Santa Cruz Island, and the guides not only helped me frame the best images, but also gave me advice on camera settings, lighting, and animal behavior. These tours might last anything from a half-day to a full week. Expect to pay between *$100 and $300* per day, depending on the tour's length and content.

Birdwatching Tours: Birdwatching is a serious activity in the Galapagos, and I strongly advise hiring a local expert if you want to view a wide variety of species. Isabela Island is an excellent place to see Darwin's finches and other rare birds, and guides will lead you through woods, coastal cliffs, and volcanic craters. San Cristóbal and Genovesa are also excellent birdwatching destinations, notably for boobies, frigatebirds, and galápagos hawks. These tours typically cost *between $60 to $150 for a half-day tour.*

Snorkeling & Marine Tours: If you want to get up close to marine life, there are guided snorkeling tours that look for sea lions, marine iguanas, and tropical fish. I went on a half-day trip of Gardner Bay, and the instructors not only pointed out species but also helped me take the perfect underwater photos. A snorkeling day tour typically costs *$75-$125.*

The Galapagos Islands are a photographer's and birdwatcher's dream come true. Whether you're looking to snap the perfect photo of a blue-footed booby or simply spending time observing

A guided tour of the island's interesting wildlife will take your experience to the next level.

The animal experience in the Galapagos Islands is incomparable, and it's one of the primary reasons why so many visitors, including me, return year after year. Meeting curious sea lions, admiring gorgeous tortoises, and witnessing breathtaking birds is a true privilege. The Galapagos Islands are a living laboratory for nature, and it is our job to maintain and protect their unique environment. By following the proper criteria and engaging in sustainable activities, we can all ensure that the beauty and wonder of these islands are preserved for future generations.

Chapter 9: Top Activities to Do in the Galapagos

9.1 Island Hopping: Discovering the Archipelago's Most Beautiful Islands

The Galapagos Islands are a large archipelago of 13 major islands, each with its own unique appeal, so island hopping is an essential element of any vacation here. One of the most exciting aspects of the vacation for me was the journey between these islands. Each island provided something fresh, whether it was a distinct environment, a different variety of wildlife, or a quieter, more secluded hideaway.

Santa Cruz Island

This is where most tourists begin their Galapagos trip, and for good reason. It is home to Puerto Ayora, the main town, and the famous *Charles Darwin Research Station,* which I highly recommend visiting. Santa Cruz also has the gorgeous Tortuga Bay, which offers a wonderful combination of tranquil beach time and wildlife encounters.

Sierra Negra Volcano

Isabela Island:

Known for its magnificent volcanic scenery, Isabela offers close encounters with giant tortoises, exploration of the *Sierra Negra volcano,* and relaxation on some of the Galapagos' greatest beaches. The area is alive with sea lions and penguins, and I spent many afternoons simply watching them bask in the sun.

San Cristóbal Island

Galápagos Interpretation Center: *San Cristóbal Island* strikes the ideal blend between local culture and natural beauty. The Galapagos Interpretation Center provided an in-depth look into the islands' history, and the neighboring *Kicker Rock* was one of my favorite snorkeling places for sea lions and beautiful fish.

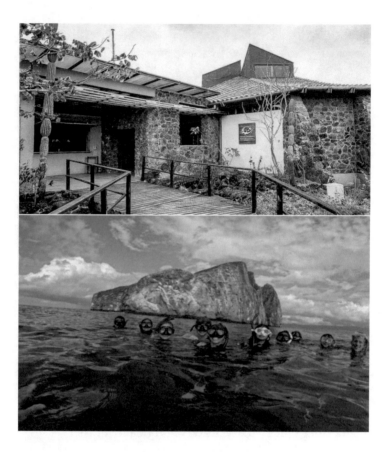

Floreana Island:

One of the quietest islands, Floreana is frequently missed, but its Post Office Bay (where sailors used to leave mail for others to pick up) and the ***Devil's Crown*** (a popular snorkeling area) made it one of my favorite visits.

Island hopping in the Galapagos allows you to view the archipelago's full range, from bustling towns to serene, unspoiled beaches, and I recommend spending at least 4-7 days exploring a selection of the islands. Regular boat rides or short flights between the islands make getting from one to the next easy.

9.2 Snorkelling, Scuba Diving, and Beach Days

If there is one thing that truly distinguishes the Galapagos Islands, it is the opportunity to plunge into its pristine seas and explore the underwater world. I've been to numerous coastal destinations, but nothing beats the snorkeling and diving adventures in the Galapagos. The seas here are rich in biodiversity, with crystal-clear clarity and a diverse range of marine life that cannot be found anyplace else on Earth.

Snorkeling: Whether you're a beginner or a seasoned snorkeler, the Galapagos has some of the world's most rewarding snorkeling destinations. One of my highlights was snorkeling at *Devil's Crown (off Floreana Island).* It's a submerged volcanic cone where currents bring in a variety of aquatic life, including sharks, rays, and schools of fish that appear to shine in the sun.

Española Island

Gardner Bay on *Española Island* was a wonderful experience, where I could swim with curious sea lions who would dart about me and playfully bite at my fins. It was an unforgettable experience, especially because the sea lions seemed to want to direct the show!

Wolf and Darwin Islands

Scuba Diving: For those who prefer to explore deeper, the Galapagos Islands are one of the world's best scuba diving locations. The diverse marine ecosystems here include hammerhead sharks, manta rays, sea turtles, and schools of colorful fish. The Wolf and Darwin Islands, located on the archipelago's northernmost tip, are regarded as the best diving destinations, however journeys to these islands are frequently more expensive and require longer stays. I was fortunate enough to participate in a live aboard dive tour that allowed me access to these secluded islands. The pleasure of diving alongside whale sharks and watching hammerheads swim by was above my expectations.

Tortuga Bay

Beach Days: After the diving thrills, the Galapagos' beaches provide an opportunity to relax. The sand is often powdery white or golden, and the beaches are rarely crowded. My favorite was Tortuga Bay on Santa Cruz, where the tranquil turquoise waters and pure white sand provided the ideal retreat. There are also beautiful beaches on *Isabela* and *San Cristóbal* where you may spend a relaxing day reading, swimming, or simply taking in the scenery.

9.3 Hiking, Kayaking, and Exploring Volcanoes

The Galapagos Islands are not only about water; they also provide excellent chances for hiking and exploring on land. The volcanic topography, which includes craters, lava fields, and verdant mountains, provides breathtaking views and an immersive experience.

San Cristóbal

Hiking Volcanoes: One of my favorite climbs was to the summit of **Sierra Negra** on Isabela Island, home to one of the world's largest active volcanoes. The climb is difficult but well worth it for the breathtaking views of the surrounding islands and the massive caldera. The **Lobería Trail** near *San Cristóbal* offers a trip through coastal woodlands with opportunities to observe wildlife and volcanic phenomena.

Kayaking: Kayaking is a relaxing and satisfying way to explore the islands, particularly their shoreline. I enjoyed kayaking in the tranquil waters of Santa Cruz and Isabela, where I frequently observed marine life such as sea turtles and stingrays glide beneath me. The best part is that you can do this nearly anywhere on the islands, making it an ideal activity to perform with a partner or by yourself.

Lava Tubes & Lava Flows: If you're interested in the islands' geological wonders, go to Santa Cruz to see the lava tubes. These tunnels, created by flowing lava, are a remarkable natural phenomenon. I had the opportunity to visit several of them, and it seemed like entering a secret underground world—quiet and cool, but curiously intriguing.

9.4 Day trips and expeditions from Charles Darwin Station to Tortuga Bay.

For those who have limited time or prefer to stay on one island, there are various great day trips and excursions available that will allow you to explore the finest of the Galapagos. These excursions frequently center on certain activities, such as wildlife viewing, beach exploration, or educational visits.

Charles Darwin Research Station

The Charles Darwin Research Station on **Santa Cruz Island** is a must-see for anyone interested in learning more about the Galapagos' conservation efforts. The station provides an educational experience in which visitors may learn about the islands' ecosystems, the famed giant tortoises, and the continuing preservation efforts designed to safeguard the archipelago's distinctive species.

Tortuga Bay is one of the Galapagos' most picturesque beaches, located near **Puerto Ayora on Santa Cruz.** To get to this beautiful length of sand, kayak or walk along a mangrove-lined trail. Once there, you'll be greeted to crystal-clear seas ideal for swimming, snorkeling, or simply relaxing.

Day Trips to Nearby Islands: For those with limited time, various short excursions can be taken from the main islands. I definitely recommend a boat trip to North Seymour Island for birdwatching, or a trip to Santa Fe to observe the rare land iguanas and the beautiful bay ideal for snorkeling. These day trips allow you to enjoy the beauty of more distant islands without having to stay the night.

9.5 Hidden Gems: Off the Beaten Path Activities You Can't Miss

While the Galapagos are well-known for their major tourist sites, there are a number of hidden jewels and lesser-known locations that are well worth seeing. If you're wanting to escape the crowds and uncover something unique, I highly recommend the following off-the-beaten-path activities:

Bartholomew Island:

This small island, which many people overlook, is well-known for its breathtaking vistas of *Pinnacle Rock* as well as its peculiar, unearthly terrain. A trek to the summit of the island provides amazing views.

Genovesa Island,

sometimes known as *"Bird Island,"* is a popular birdwatching destination. It's not a usual tourist destination, but the Red-footed Booby colonies and frigatebird nests make it a must-see for avian **wildlife enthusiasts.**

Gardner Bay on Española Island is a popular snorkeling area, although visiting early in the morning can provide a serene experience. The bay is home to a big colony of sea lions, and I had the rare opportunity to swim with them nearly alone.

Floreana Island's Post Office Bay: Visiting Post Office Bay is like going back in time. This historical site, once used to carry mail by whalers in the 18th century, is now a pleasant interactive stop for tourists. You can put a postcard in the mailbox, and if you're lucky, someone will pick it up and personally deliver it to the receiver.

The Galapagos Islands offer a variety of unique activities, and whether you prefer wildlife watching, trekking, or simply taking in the natural splendor, there is something for everyone. Some of my favorite memories were made in the quieter parts of these islands, where I could appreciate the natural environment in its purest form. The key is to venture beyond the well-trodden pathways, and you'll discover that the actual splendor of the Galapagos awaits just around the bend.

Chapter 10: Nightlife and Entertainment on the Galapagos

10.1 Where to go After Dark: bars, restaurants, and live music.

While the Galapagos Islands are well-known for their magnificent natural beauty and fauna, visitors may be surprised to learn that the archipelago also has a surprising number of nightlife alternatives for those wishing to unwind after a day of adventure.

During my time in the Galapagos, I discovered that the nightlife is more laid-back than in bustling cities, but it's ideal for individuals looking for a relaxing and unique evening. The environment is frequently relaxed and welcoming, with many bars and restaurants providing open-air seating where you can enjoy the evening breeze while soaking up the island vibe.

Puerto Ayora (Santa Cruz Island) is the largest town in the Galapagos and the center of the archipelago's nightlife. There are plenty of taverns, pubs, and restaurants that stay open late. One of my favorite places is The Rock, a vibrant pub and restaurant on the ocean. It's the ideal place to have a nice beer or beverage while watching the boats pass by and listening to some relaxing music. The pub frequently showcases local live music performances, ranging from acoustic guitar settings to Latin jazz, making for an enjoyable evening out.

Isabela Island: If you're vacationing on Isabela Island, *La Casa de Marita* is a lovely beachside restaurant with a welcoming atmosphere. While it is not a crazy nightlife destination, it does provide a relaxing ambiance in which you may enjoy a cocktail by the ocean while listening to the waves. For a more lively ambiance, *Bar El Barón* has a wonderful assortment of beverages and the occasional live music session featuring local musicians performing famous Latin tunes.

San Cristóbal Island: The major town, *Puerto Baquerizo Moreno*, has a variety of modest, laid-back bars that come alive in the evenings. *Muyu's Bar* is popular among both residents and tourists. The modest, friendly venue serves delicious beverages and frequently showcases live musicians doing everything from salsa to reggae. It's a terrific spot to meet locals, hear stories from fisherman and tourists, and soak in the island's warm, tropical atmosphere.

Live Music and Events: Although the islands may not have the same level of nightlife as larger cities, I spent some wonderful nights listening to live music. Local musicians frequently perform at casual coastal establishments, creating an ideal setting for a peaceful evening. *Alaea Bar* on Isabela Island is one of these venues where you can hear local and regional live music, ranging from energetic salsa to peaceful acoustic shows. It is an excellent approach to immerse oneself in the island's cultural rhythm.

10.2 Local Activities, Festivals, and Cultural Experiences

While the Galapagos are well-known for their animals and pristine scenery, they also have a rich cultural legacy, which is evident in their festivals, local gatherings, and celebrations. If you're fortunate enough to visit during one of the islands' yearly celebrations, you'll get a taste of the lively local culture and customs that determine life here.

Carnival (February): One of the Galapagos' most anticipated occasions is Carnival, a holiday celebrated throughout the islands with parades, music, dancing, and street parties. Carnival celebrations in Santa Cruz are a colorful spectacle, with elaborate costumes and music filling the streets. During my stay, I had the opportunity to participate in one of the parades, which was a fantastic event full of exciting acts and infectious energy. If you're on the islands at this period, attend the events to get a taste of local culture.

Fiestas de la Virgen del Carmen (July): The Fiestas de la Virgen del Carmen are a week-long celebration in Puerto Ayora honoring the Galapagos Islands' patron saint. The celebration features processions, traditional dances, music, and feasts, providing a colorful and engaging experience. During my visit, I joined the residents in a lively march and was treated to a cultural showcase that emphasized the islands' indigenous and colonial heritage. The event's joyful atmosphere and community spirit make it a must-see for visitors looking to get a taste of local life outside of beaches and wildlife.

Isabela Island's Fiestas Patronales (August): The yearly Fiestas Patronales on Isabela Island is another excellent festival, particularly for those interested in learning about local traditions and customs. The island's major town, Puerto Villamil, is bustling with food booths, music, and games, and the streets are alive with laughter and enthusiasm. I had a great time witnessing the traditional dances and participating in the activities, which provided an excellent opportunity to mingle with both locals and other travelers.

Cultural Activities & Workshops: In addition to festivals, there are year-round chances to participate with local culture. Many islands include workshops where you can learn traditional crafts, such as those manufactured from native materials like wood and shells. I attended a local painting school on *San Cristóbal Island,* where the artist taught us how to paint the Galapagos' unique scenery and wildlife. These cultural activities provide an excellent opportunity to learn about the local way of life while supporting local craftsmen and creators.

10.3 Quiet Spots to Stargaze

After days of exploring, nothing beats the serene quiet of Galapagos nights. The islands' secluded location, along with low light pollution, makes an ideal atmosphere for stargazing. There's something genuinely magical about observing the night sky above the Pacific, away from the lights and distractions of contemporary life. Here are some of my favorite stargazing places that I discovered while in the Galapagos:

Tortuga Bay (Santa Cruz Island): One of the most peaceful areas to watch the night sky is Tortuga Bay on Santa Cruz Island. The bay is secluded and has little to no artificial illumination, making it an excellent place to see the stars. I recall sitting on the beach with a bottle of wine, gazing up at the endless amount of stars glittering above. The sight of the Milky Way arching across the night sky was breathtaking, and it felt as if the world had slowed down, allowing me to appreciate the enormity of the universe.

Isabela Island's Highlands: For an even more private experience, visit Isabela Island's highlands, where the night sky appears to stretch forever. The location is tranquil and absent of significant light sources, providing an excellent opportunity to observe constellations and planets with minimal interference from city lights. I made the short trip up to an isolated area above Puerto Villamil and was rewarded with a breathtaking view of the stars.

Because of the islands' peculiar location in the Pacific, stargazing here feels out of this world.

San Cristóbal Island: The peaceful beaches of Puerto Baquerizo Moreno on San Cristóbal Island provide excellent astronomy chances. After a day of activity, I discovered a calm location on Punta Carola Beach, just a short walk from the main town. The calm murmur of the waves and the huge, untouched night sky above provided the ideal setting for me to think on my vacation and admire the islands' natural beauty.

The Sierra Negra Crater (Isabela Island): For an incredible stargazing experience, hike up to the Sierra Negra Volcano on Isabela Island at night. The viewpoint provides sweeping views of the island and the water below, and the night sky is ideal for astronomy. The solitude and elevation make this a genuinely unique location for catching a glimpse of meteor showers or planets on a clear night.

While the Galapagos Islands are most renowned for their daytime activities and magnificent wildlife, the archipelago also has a distinct and peaceful nocturnal scene. Whether you're listening to live music on the waterfront, partying with the locals at a festival, or stargazing beneath the huge Pacific sky, the Galapagos Islands are more than just a nature lover's paradise. The islands' combination of tranquil quiet areas, vibrant local culture, and laid-back nightlife make them ideal for unwinding after a day of exploring and experiencing a slower, more connected way of life.

Chapter 11: The Galapagos for Solo Travelers.

13.1 How I Navigated the Islands Solo: Tips and Insights Traveling alone through the Galapagos Islands was one of the most fulfilling experiences I've ever had. The archipelago, with its unspoiled beauty and unusual animals, is ideal for those seeking isolation and a closer connection to nature. But, of course, traveling alone necessitates more planning and a spirit of adventure. Here's how I navigated the islands alone, and how you can too.

Ease of Travel: One of my favorite aspects of traveling solo in the Galapagos was how easy it was to move about. The islands, despite their isolated location, are well-equipped for independent travel. Public transportation is efficient, with regular ferries between islands and reasonably priced taxis on each of the major islands. I discovered that Puerto Ayora on Santa Cruz Island acted as the principal hub for transport between the islands, and once I sorted out the ferry timetable, I was able to get around effortlessly. The ferry system is safe and reliable, making it ideal for island hopping on your own.

Accommodation possibilities for Solo Travelers: There are numerous possibilities for solo travelers, including inexpensive hostels and private eco-lodges. During my trip, I preferred to stay in tiny guesthouses or boutique hotels, where I could meet other travelers while still getting the solitude and quiet I needed. On Isabela Island, I stayed at a wonderful eco-lodge where the owner not only provided me advice on the island but also introduced me to other solo travelers. I've discovered that smaller lodgings are ideal for meeting people without being overwhelmed by crowds or groups.

Guided Tours for Solo Travelers: As a solo traveler, I frequently attended small group tours, particularly for activities such as snorkeling, hiking, and wildlife viewing. These trips are well-organized and provide an opportunity to meet other like-minded visitors while yet having a personalized experience. On Santa Cruz, I went on a day trip to Tortuga Bay with a local guide. The group was small and intimate, making it an excellent opportunity to engage with others while learning about the island's nature. These smaller groups provided greater flexibility, and the guides were always willing to offer their knowledge, improving the trip even further.

Enjoying Nature on Your Own Terms: One of the most appealing parts of solo travel in the Galapagos is the ability to explore at your own leisure. Whether climbing in Sierra Negra or diving off the coast of Isabela, the islands provide several options for personal exploration. I discovered that having no predetermined schedule allowed me to spend as much time as I wanted at a scenic spot or a peaceful beach without feeling rushed. I spent a day alone at Gardner Bay on Española Island, fully engrossed in its quiet beauty. There's something quite tranquil. about being alone in nature in such a remote and pure setting.

11.2 Safety Tips and the Best Places to Meet Other Travelers

Traveling alone in the Galapagos is generally safe. The islands are small, with close-knit villages, and tourism is the primary industry, so you'll constantly find other travelers and pleasant residents nearby. However, as with any vacation, there are a few things to bear in mind to ensure a successful trip.

Safety First: Although I always felt safe in the Galapagos, there are a few practical practices that helped me feel more secure. First, always tell someone where you're going. It's always a good idea to share your daily schedule with your hotel, a local guide, or another traveler. The islands are small, but if you plan on doing any remote hiking or swimming, you should be prepared. Make sure your phone is charged and that you have all of the required supplies, such as water, food, and sunscreen.

Health and Hygiene: The islands are a safe area to visit, but as with any remote location, it is critical to take health precautions. I made careful to bring a modest first-aid box with basic prescriptions and personal stuff such as hand sanitizer. Drink only bottled or purified water to avoid problems. I also carried my own reusable water bottle, which I filled at filtered stations in several locations.

Meeting Other Travellers: Solo travel does not have to entail being alone the entire time! While the Galapagos is recognized for its tranquil, lonely setting, there are numerous social options. Puerto Ayora on Santa Cruz Island is ideal for meeting other visitors, especially in the nights. After a day of adventure, I frequently found myself speaking with other solo travelers at The Rock Bar, a popular hangout for both tourists and locals looking to unwind with drinks and live music. The informal atmosphere of the bars and restaurants makes it easy to pick up conversation.

Social excursions and Activities: Group excursions are an excellent way to meet other single travelers. The Galapagos Islands have several group excursions, ranging from day tours to Devil's Crown for snorkeling to full-day hikes up volcanoes. These trips allow you to meet other guests while participating in the island's activities. I joined a group for a kayaking adventure around Tortuga Bay, and it was a great chance to meet others who shared my passion for the outdoors.

Social Accommodations: Hostels and guesthouses are another excellent method to meet new people. During my stay in San Cristóbal, I slept in a tiny guesthouse with a communal kitchen and lounge room, where I could talk with other visitors from all over the world. The relaxed atmosphere provided an ideal setting for sharing insights, exchanging experiences, and even planning the next day's travels.

11.3 Solo Adventures: Finding Peace on the Islands.

One of the most valuable benefits of solo travel is the chance to achieve inner calm and enjoy the quiet. The Galapagos Islands, with their pristine beauty and calm landscapes, provided the ideal backdrop for me to ponder, relax, and appreciate nature at my own speed.

Solitude in Nature: Whether I was wandering the calm roads of Isabela's Highlands, going up to the Sierra Negra Volcano, or watching the sunset on a remote beach on San Cristóbal, I discovered that the islands allowed me to actually be present in the moment. One of my favorite experiences was going to Tortuga Bay. The bay, noted for its crystal-clear waters and white beach, felt like a personal oasis. I spent hours walking along the beach, alone with my thoughts and watching sea turtles glide by. The natural rhythm of the islands is very revitalizing, and I discovered that the more I submerged myself in solitude, the more attached I felt to the location.

Hiking and Reflection: The Galapagos also has various tranquil hiking routes that are ideal for reflection. I spent a day hiking around Santa Cruz Island's Galapagos National Park, passing through lush woods and volcanic craters with only the sounds of birds and wind rustling through the trees for company. Hiking alone provided me with the opportunity to reflect deeply while also taking in the breathtaking scenery that surrounding me. It was a period of seclusion that I will not forget.

Spiritual Moments: If you're looking for a peaceful area to reflect or simply connect with nature, consider visiting El Junco Lagoon on San Cristóbal Island. The trip to the lagoon is a peaceful one, and the scene of the quiet water against the backdrop of foggy mountains is almost surreal. The calm of the location made it ideal for meditation and thought, and I spent hours simply admiring the view, feeling at ease with the world around me.

Solo travel in the Galapagos is a unique experience. The islands provide an ideal balance of excitement and tranquility, allowing you to interact with nature in a truly personal way. Whether you want to meet other visitors or find refuge in nature, the Galapagos gives you the freedom to create your own experience. Solo travel here was not only simple, but also quite rewarding—it allowed me to explore at my own pace, meet intriguing people, and make amazing memories along the way.

Chapter 12: Itinerary Suggestions

14.1 A 7-Day Adventure in the Galapagos

A week in the Galapagos provides an ideal blend of discovery, excitement, and leisure. With 7 days, you may visit the main islands, see the archipelago's distinctive animals, and soak up the natural splendor. Here's how I spent my seven-day adventure, and how you can make the most of yours.

Day 1: Arrival at Baltra and Santa Cruz Island.

Arrive on **Baltra Island,** the major gateway to the Galapagos, and take a short ferry journey to Santa Cruz Island. I spent my first day relaxing and exploring Puerto Ayora, the island's largest town. After checking into my accommodations, I went to the **Charles Darwin Research Station** to hear about conservation efforts and the iconic Galapagos tortoises. A stroll down the waterfront at nightfall provided an ideal introduction to the island.

Day 2: Tortuga Bay and Santa Cruz Highlands.

Start your day early by taking a boat to Tortuga Bay, a beautiful beach with white sand and turquoise waters.

This location is perfect for kayaking, and I got the opportunity to paddle out to Iguana Island and observe wildlife up close. In the afternoon, visit the Santa Cruz Highlands to explore the volcanic sceneries and see wild tortoises in their natural environment. The highlands are lush and vibrant, providing a stark contrast to the island's barren coastal parts.

Day 3: Isabela Island.

Take the early ferry to Isabela, the archipelago's largest island. The drive takes around two hours, and once there, I recommend going straight to **Puerto Villamil** to rest and explore. Then, climb to the **Wall of Tears**, a historical landmark with breathtaking views of the island. In the evening, head to **Concha de Perla** for a relaxing snorkel with sea lions, penguins, and tropical fish.

Day 4: Sierra Negra Volcano and Tintoreras.

Isabela Island is home to the **Sierra Negra Volcano**, one of the Galapagos' most active volcanoes. The trek to the summit provides panoramic views of the island and its massive caldera. Next, board a boat to **Tintoreras,** a small series of islands off the coast. The waters here are filled with marine life, and I saw sharks, rays, and sea lions while snorkeling.

Day 5: San Cristóbal Island.

Take a morning ferry to **San Cristóbal Island,** which is recognized for its rugged beauty and rich history. Spend the day at **Kicker Rock,** a stunning rock formation where you can snorkel alongside sea lions, sharks, and massive schools of fish. In the afternoon, visit **Puerto Baquerizo Moreno,** the Galapagos capital, and walk along **La Lobería Beach,** where I saw joyful sea lions basking on the coast.

Day 6: Española Island and Gardner Bay.

Take a day trip to Española Island, one of the archipelago's oldest and most biologically varied. I spent the morning in Gardner Bay, a beautiful beach with perfect white sand, and **Punta Suarez,** which is famed for its wildlife and magnificent rocks. Española is known for its marine iguanas, blue-footed boobies, and albatross colonies, which I had the opportunity to see firsthand.

Day 7: Return to Santa Cruz and Departure

On your final day, return to Santa Cruz Island for any last-minute activities, such as a trip to **Garrapatero Beach** or a kayaking tour of Academy Bay. Take a leisurely lunch at one of the town's best restaurants before heading to the airport for your return trip to the mainland.

This 7-day itinerary offers a thorough taste of the Galapagos Islands, combining active exploration with times of rest to deliver a well-rounded perspective of the archipelago's fauna, beaches, and volcanic scenery.

12.2 Three days in the Galapagos: A Quick and Intense Getaway

If you just have three days to tour the Galapagos, you'll want to make the most of them. While there isn't enough time to see all of the islands, you can still experience the best of the Galapagos in a short yet intense vacation. Here's how I made the most of my three-day visit and how you can, too.

Day 1: Santa Cruz Island.

Arrive on **Baltra Island** and transport to Santa Cruz. Begin your tour by visiting Tortuga Bay, where you can kayak and snorkel with marine turtles and lively sea lions. In the afternoon, go to the Charles Darwin Research Station to learn about conservation activities on the islands. If you have time, visit Los Gemelos in the highlands to witness volcanic craters and wild tortoises.

Day 2 - Isabela Island

On your second day, catch an early ferry to Isabela Island. Once there, **explore Tintoreras,** a little islet inhabited by white-tipped reef sharks, marine iguanas, and sea lions. The hike up to the Sierra Negra Volcano was the highlight of my day, as it provided amazing views of the island's enormous volcanic environment. For a more leisurely afternoon, relax on Puerto Villamil's tranquil beaches or take a boat excursion to nearby Las Tintoreras.

Day 3: San Cristobal Island

On your final day, board a ferry to **San Cristóbal Island.** Head directly to **Kicker Rock** for a morning of snorkeling. The clear seas are rich with marine life such as sea lions, sharks, and rays. Then, spend the afternoon exploring the island's historic sites, such as the Interpretation Center, which provides vital information on the islands' history and conservation activities. End your vacation with a tranquil stroll along **La Lobería Beach,** where you can see sea lions sunbathe in the sun.

This fast route allows you to see three of the main islands, each with its own unique animals and sceneries. While it's fast-paced, there are enough of great moments to make your three-day trip unforgettable.

12.3 My Recommended Two-Week Itinerary for the Best Galapagos Experience

For those fortunate enough to spend two weeks in the Galapagos, this is the ideal opportunity to thoroughly immerse themselves in the islands' beauties. With two weeks, you can tour a range of islands, observe varied fauna, and participate in the archipelago's many activities. Here's how I spent my two weeks in the Galapagos, along with my recommendation for the ideal plan.

Day 1–3: Santa Cruz Island

Arrive at **Baltra Island** and travel to Santa Cruz, where your Galapagos experience begins. Spend a few days discovering the island's beaches, hills, and wildlife. Don't miss **Tortuga Bay, Charles Darwin Research Station**, and a trip through the Santa Cruz Highlands to witness giant tortoises in their native setting. **Garrapatero Beach** is also a good place to go kayaking and bird watching.

Day 4–5: Isabela Island

Take the ferry to Isabela Island. Spend your first day relaxing and enjoying the laid-back atmosphere of Puerto Villamil. On day 5, take a full-day excursion to **Sierra Negra Volcano** for a strenuous but rewarding walk, or spend the day snorkeling around **Tintoreras** and discovering the abundant marine life. You could alternatively spend a more leisurely day at **Concha de Perla,** where I enjoyed snorkeling with sea lions.

Day 6–7: Española Island.

Española Island is an ideal destination for bird enthusiasts. The island is noted for its blue-footed boobies and albatross colonies. Spend two days on **Española**, visiting **Gardner Bay** for a beach day and

Punta Suarez for a bird-watching hike. Don't forget to look for the colorful marine iguanas that call this island home.

Day 8–9: San Cristóbal Island

Take the ferry to San Cristóbal Island and spend a few days exploring. Explore the island by hiking to **El Junco Lagoon,** snorkeling at **Kicker Rock,** and relaxing on **La Lobería's** quieter beaches. **The Interpretation Center** is a great place to learn about the islands' history, while Cerro Tijeretas provides an excellent birdwatching opportunity.

Day 10–11: Floreana Island

Take a boat to Floreana Island, which is less touristic and has a fascinating mix of history and animals. Visit the old post office barrel, snorkel in the clear seas, and enjoy the unspoiled beaches. Devil's Crown, a submerged volcanic crater, is one of the best snorkeling places in the Galapagos, with abundant fish and marine life.

Day 12–14: Santa Cruz and Departure

Return to Santa Cruz Island for your final few days. Make a final day trip to Plazas Island.

Alternatively, North Seymour Island offers an outstanding nature encounter. These islands are densely populated with nesting birds, especially frigate birds and boobies. Spend your final day shopping for gifts in Puerto Ayora while thinking on your fantastic experience. Take one more swim in the pristine blue seas before boarding your trip back to the mainland.

This two-week trip is ideal for those looking to see everything the Galapagos has to offer, from iconic species to distant, pristine islands. It offers both adventure and relaxation, allowing you to connect closely with nature in one of the world's most remarkable places.

Chapter 13: Leaving the Islands: Reflections and Travel Tips for the Return Trip

13.1 Takeaways from My Galapagos Experience

As I boarded the plane back to the mainland following my time in the Galapagos, I found myself reflecting on everything I had seen and done. The islands had a way of transforming me, delivering something far more than just a vacation. The time spent in this remarkable corner of the earth felt like a spiritual and sensual retreat.

The Galapagos Islands are more than just a haven for nature; they serve as a reminder of what is possible when the natural world is safeguarded and valued. From the slow-moving tortoises to the joyful sea lions and the faraway calls of the blue-footed boobies, the wildlife I saw felt unlike anything else on Earth. In these vast, pure landscapes, I felt a connection to something far bigger than myself—a reminder of the delicate balance we must strike between the natural world and our modern way of life.

The most important takeaway for me was how much we still have to learn from these islands. The Galapagos Islands were more than just a lovely getaway; they were also a living laboratory. Every nook seemed to teach a lesson about evolution, conservation, and the interdependence of life. Spending time in such a location increased my awareness of the delicate threads that connect the world's ecosystems. The Galapagos was memorable not only for the creatures and sceneries, but also for the profound sense of place—the overwhelming impression that I was in a rare and unique corner of the world that still runs on its own terms.

In addition to the beautiful animals, the islands instilled in me a strong sense of thankfulness. The Galapagos Islands remind you of the beauty of simplicity—nature's capacity to produce balance, harmony, and breathtaking sights without the need for human intervention. Every stride, every connection with the animals, and every peaceful time by the sea felt like a unique treasure.

13.2 How to Bring the Islands' Spirit Home with You

It was bittersweet to leave the Galapagos, but I knew I could keep the spirit of the islands with me. Although literally transporting the Galapagos to your everyday life is hard, there are ways to keep the islands' allure alive long after you leave. Here are some personal suggestions for taking that sense of tranquility, adventure, and connection to nature back home.

Embrace Sustainable Travel Practices: One of the most important lessons I learned from my time in the Galapagos was the value of sustainability. The islands' tight tourism laws have helped them to remain pristine, and I've attempted to adopt more sustainable habits into my daily life since returning. Whether it's limiting plastic use, supporting eco-friendly businesses, or lobbying for conservation activities in my neighborhood, I've made it a point to uphold the responsible travel values I learnt in the Galapagos.

Animals Appreciation: The Galapagos taught me the importance of appreciating and respecting animals. I've become more aware of the animals I see in my daily life, whether it's watching birds in my neighborhood or helping local wildlife charity. The islands instilled in me a love of wildlife that is more than just intrigue; it serves as a reminder to respect and protect the species with whom we share this planet.

Stay Connected to Nature: The connection I felt with the natural world in the Galapagos does not have to end when I leave the islands. Since returning, I've made a concerted effort to spend more time in nature, whether through hikes, trips to national parks, or simply strolling through local green spaces. The peace and calmness I felt in the Galapagos were unsurpassed, and I strive to recover some of that calm whenever possible by reconnecting with nature.

Support Conservation Efforts: The Galapagos' conservation efforts demonstrate what can be accomplished when we prioritize environmental protection. Since my visit, I've become involved in local conservation programs and made donations to wildlife preservation projects. The islands showed me the power of good change, which I've taken with me as active support for environmental concerns.

Share Your Experience: Sharing your story with others is one of the most effective methods to keep the Galapagos spirit alive. I've discovered that talking about my experience on the islands with friends and family not only helps to keep the memories alive, but also raises awareness about the necessity of safeguarding such locations. Sharing the beauty of the Galapagos, whether through social media posts, blog writing, or informal conversations, can help preserve the islands' essence for future generations to enjoy.

13.3 Final Thoughts: Is the Galapagos Still Worth It in 2025

As I look on my time in the Galapagos, I can certainly state that the islands remain one of the most amazing places on Earth, both in 2025 and beyond. Yes, the archipelago has issues, including climate change and the strains of increasing tourism. Despite these obstacles, the Galapagos continue to provide something extremely unusual and valuable: an undisturbed ecosystem in which wildlife thrives in ways that appear almost otherworldly.

In 2025, the Galapagos Islands are as breathtaking as ever. Wildlife still thrives in its native environment, and the landscapes continue to captivate with their stark beauty. The marine life beneath the seas, the verdant highlands, the stark lava fields, and the beautiful beaches—each corner of these islands feels like a living witness to nature's grandeur.

For travelers in 2025, the Galapagos Islands are a must-see for anyone who wishes to see life in its most natural, unspoiled form. Whether you're a wildlife enthusiast, an adventurer, or simply looking to immerse yourself in nature's grandeur, the Galapagos Islands have something special to offer. However, as a visitor, it is critical to respect the islands and promote sustainable tourism. By visiting responsibly and adhering to conservation guidelines, we may help maintain this living laboratory for future generations.

If you've been debating whether or not to visit the Galapagos, I can assure you that the trip is well worth it. It's more than simply a journey; it's an experience that will change the way you see the world and your place within it. Whether you're exploring the wildlife, trekking the volcanic trails, or simply relaxing on the islands, the Galapagos will be with you long after you leave. And as we approach 2025 and beyond, the Galapagos Islands will remain a beacon of natural beauty and a reminder of the necessity of environmental protection.

The islands may be distant, but the values they teach are universal: appreciate nature, protect wildlife, and live in harmony with the world around you. The Galapagos are more than just a destination; they are a voyage into the heart of the Earth's natural wonders, waiting for you to discover them.

Appendix A: Contacts and Resources

When arranging a vacation to the Galapagos, having the appropriate contacts and resources at your disposal can make a big difference. The following is a list of crucial contacts and resources to aid you along your journey:

The Galapagos National Park Service's official website provides current regulations, permits, and environmental policies. www.galapagos.gob.ec
Call +593 5 252 2929 or email info@galapagos.gob.ec.

Galápagos Tourism Board

For basic information about visiting the Galapagos, including lodgings and attractions:
Visit www.galapagos.travel, call +593 2 394 1234, or send an email to info@galapagos.travel.

Charles Darwin Research Station

For more information on conservation programs, educational tours, and open hours:
Website: www.darwinfoundation.org.
For inquiries, please contact +593 5 252 6021 or email info@darwinfoundation.org.

Local airlines that offer flights to the Galapagos.

AeroGal (www.aerogal.com.ec)
TAME Airlines (www.tame.com.ec)
Ecuador Airlines (www.flyecuador.com.ec)
In Ecuador, the emergency contact for ambulances is 911.
Dial 101 for police, 102 for fire, and +593 5 252 2265 for the Galapagos emergency hotline.

B. Galapagos Travel Vocabulary

Knowing a few important Spanish phrases will help you have a more enjoyable trip to the Galapagos. Here are some simple terminology and phrases that will help you communicate.
¡Hola! - Hello!
How much does it cost? How much does it cost?
Please, gracias, and por favor.
Where is the bathroom located? - Where is the bathroom?
Agua refers to water, while comida is food.
Isla - Island
Tortuga – Tortoise

León marino - Sea Lion
Buceo – Diving
Snorkel- Snorkeling
Do you speak English? - Can you speak English?
Ayuda - Help.
Emergencia - Emergency.
Reserva Natural - Nature Reserve
Tour Guiado - Guided Tour

C. Packing List for the Galapagos.

Packing for the Galapagos necessitates a combination of pragmatism and preparation for many conditions, ranging from beach days to excursions across volcanic terrain. Here's a checklist to guarantee you don't forget anything important:

Documents and Essentials

- Passport (at least 6 months valid)
- Travel insurance details
- Airline tickets and hotel reservations
- Visa (if applicable to your nationality)
- Copies of vital documents.

Clothing

Lightweight and breathable clothing (tropical environment)
Comfortable hiking shoes
Flip-flops or sandals for the beach
Swimsuit(s)

Light jacket or sweater (for cool evenings)
Hat, sunglasses, and sunscreen
Rain jacket (for unexpected rainfall).
Long pants and long-sleeved shirts (for hiking and mosquito prevention)

Gear & Accessories

- Waterproof dry bag (for expeditions and boat trips).
- Daypack (used for day travels)
- Snorkeling gear (many trips include it, but you may choose to bring your own).
- Reusable Water Bottle
- Camera (with extra memory cards and batteries)
- Binoculars for Wildlife Watching
- Travel adapter for Ecuadorian outlets (Type A and B).
- Power bank to charge electronics.
- Personal toiletries (preferably eco-friendly)

Health and Safety Items

- First aid kit (containing seasickness pills, mosquito repellent, etc.)
- Prescription drugs (as applicable)
- Sunscreen and lip balm with SPF
- Hand sanitizer
- Insect repellant (particularly for highlands and humid locations)

- Waterproof phone case (suitable for snorkeling and water activities).

D. Emergency Services and Helpful Numbers

Though the Galapagos is a generally secure area to visit, it is always prudent to be prepared for the unexpected. Keep the following numbers handy just in case:
Emergency Service (Galapagos Islands)

Ambulance: dial 911.
Police: 101.
Fire Department: 102 Emergency Hotline (Galapagos): +593 5 252 2265
For environmental situations, contact the Galapagos National Park Service at +593 5 252 2929. Additionally, local hospitals and medical services are available.

Hospital de Puerto Ayora (Santa Cruz Island): +593 5 252 0988.
Hospital de San Cristóbal (San Cristóbal Island): +593 5 252 3456.
Pharmacies

Farmacia Santa Cruz (Santa Cruz Island): +593 5 252 0432.
Contact Farmacia San Cristóbal (San Cristóbal Island) at +593 5 252 0987 for tourist assistance.

Contact the Galapagos Tourist Assistance Hotline at +593 2 394 1234 or visit one of the consulates.

US Embassy in Ecuador: www.ec.usembassy.gov.
British Embassy in Ecuador: www.gov.uk/world/organizations/british-embassy-quito.

E. A Quick Reference Budget Chart

Below is a sample budget for a typical day in the Galapagos, based on 2025 prices. Keep in mind that prices can fluctuate, especially for excursions, accommodations, and activities. However, this will give you a general idea of what to expect.

Category	Budget	Mid-Range	Luxury
Accommodation (per night)	$40 - $100	$100 - $250	$250+
Meals (per day)	$15 - $30	$30 - $60	$60+
Transportation	$10 - $30 (ferries, buses)	$30 - $50 (private transfers)	$50+ (private taxis, chartered boats)
Excursions & Tours	$50 - $150	$150 - $300	$300+
Snorkeling & Diving	$60 - $150	$150 - $300	$300+
Park Fees (National Park)	$100 - $120 (per person)	$100 - $120 (per person)	$100 - $120 (per person)
Miscellaneous (souvenirs, etc.)	$10 - $30	$30 - $70	$70+

- **Total daily estimate** (Budget): $175 - $250

- **Total daily estimate** (Mid-range): $350 - $600
- **Total daily estimate** (Luxury): $600+

By understanding the range of costs, you can tailor your trip according to your preferences, whether you're looking for a budget-friendly adventure or an indulgent luxury escape in the Galapagos.

MAP

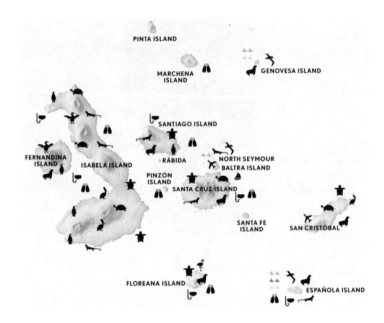

Scan for a comprehensive map of Galapagos

Scan for a live Map of Galapagos

Made in United States
Troutdale, OR
12/09/2024

26148577R00069